mosaic

mosaic

Easy indoor and outdoor weekend projects

LOUNETTE FOURIE ✻ ANITA ROSSOUW

HUMAN & ROUSSEAU
Cape Town ✻ Pretoria ✻ Johannesburg

First edition in 2004 by Human & Rousseau

40 Heerengracht, Cape Town

Copyright © published edition: Human & Rousseau (2004)

Copyright © text: Lounette Fourie & Anita Rossouw (2004)

No part of this book may be reproduced or transmitted in any form or by any means, electronic or mechanical, or by photocopying, recording or microfilming, or stored in any retrieval system, without the written permission of the publisher

Publisher – Marianne Nicol

Editor and translator – Annelene van der Merwe

Design and typesetting – Chérie Collins

Photography – Adriaan Oosthuizen

Photography assistant – Andries Joubert

Styling – Lounette Fourie and Anita Rabie

Colour separation by Virtual Colour, Cape Town

Printed and bound by Times Offset, Malaysia

ISBN 0 7981 4400 9

contents

Introduction 9
Basic equipment and materials 10
Tools 15
Choosing designs 17
Crisis management 17
Equipping your workroom 18
Cutting techniques 19
Mosaic techniques 19
Step-by-step mosaic and grouting 22

INDOOR PROJECTS

Box of coasters 28

Checkered blackboard frame 30

Two plain frames 32

Red-and-white heart 34

Plant pots 36

Key rack 38

Dishcloth hooks 40

Bread bin 42

Fridge magnets 44

Vases 46

Fruit plate with oranges 48

Mirrored trinket box 50

Cake tin 52

Teaspoon holder 54

Wine cooler 56

Jug with olives 58

Place mat 60

Towel hooks with shells and frame 62

Bathroom box 64

Tissue holder 66

Bathroom mirror 68

Butler's tray 70

Bedside cabinet 72

Mosaic chair 74

OUTDOOR PROJECTS

Glass on glass 78

Black-and-white checkered plant pot 80

Paving slabs with pebbles 82

Plate with porcelain shards 84

Birdbath 86

House number 88

Herb trough with crazy mosaic 90

Terracotta pot with glass shards 92

Shell-decorated pot 94

Sconce 96

Poolside table 98

Garden seat 100

Round table 102

LIST OF SUPPLIERS
105

BASIC DESIGNS
106

introduction

A few old shards of porcelain discovered during a holiday in the Karoo provided the inspiration for this book. We deliberated for a long time on what to do with these fragments, since there were not nearly enough of them for a complete project. They had to be supplemented with mosaic tiles – and that is how we came to be introduced to this wonderful world of colours and patterns. Instead of attending classes we read everything we could find on the subject and asked tile shops for advice. The shop assistants were exceptionally helpful and knowledgeable, and it soon became apparent that mosaic was the latest trend.

Initially this art form looked quite difficult and seemed to require a fair amount of hard physical work.

Difficult? Definitely not. Hard work? Perhaps – but undoubtedly very satisfying and worthwhile. It could be compared to tucking into a bag of sweets: once you have started, it is virtually impossible to stop. All you want is to keep on cutting and sticking down tiles.

This is one creative medium where you do not have to be a great artist in order to produce a mosaic masterpiece. No matter what you make, you will invariably feel that you have created an extraordinary work of art.

Although mosaic requires a certain technique, there are no rules. You do not have to be painstakingly accurate, study the colour wheel or be overly concerned about getting it exactly right. All you have to do is enjoy the creative process.

A short history

We regard the Spanish architect Antonio Gaudi, whose mosaics on buildings and in Parc Güell in Barcelona are truly inspiring, as the undisputed master of modern mosaic. This art form has been around for a very long time, however: mosaics dating from 400 BC were discovered in Mesopotamia. The Greeks introduced mosaic art to the world, decorating their temple floors with Greek motifs and patterns. It was subsequently adopted and developed by the Romans, especially in Rome and Pompeii. Initially mosaic was used mainly on floors, but subsequently it was employed to adorn the walls of houses, temples and baths. Marble, clay, natural stone, glass and even gold and silver were the materials used.

Basic equipment and materials

Mosaic mediums

When choosing a medium, first determine whether it will be suitable for the surface to be decorated. If the surface is meant to bear foot traffic (like our paving slabs) the mosaic medium must be tough and durable, such as pebbles, and not shells or glass; if the surface has to be even (like our tables) all the tiles must be of equal thickness; if the article is intended for outdoor use it has to be weatherproof – the cement and grout used for plant pots should therefore be waterproof. Bear in mind also that mosaic adds considerable weight to an article, which means that the background to which it will be applied has to be quite tough.

Mosaic tiles: Nowadays a vast array of local and imported mosaic tiles in every conceivable colour is freely available at tile shops. These tiles are each about 2

cm square and come attached to 30 cm square sheets. Some hobby and tile shops also sell tiles in bags. It is a good idea to stock up on tiles regularly in order to build up a wide range of colours, so that there is no need to buy an entire sheet of tiles for projects requiring only a few shades. Before starting on a larger project, it is advisable to calculate the number of tiles (plus extras) needed in each colour and to buy all the tiles at once to avoid colour variations between different dye lots.

The cost of mosaic tiles is usually determined by their colour. Black and bright colours such as red and orange are more expensive than, for instance, blue, green and grey shades, which are commonly used for swimming pools. Imported glass tiles in shades of gold, silver and perlemoen are the most expensive.

Although all mosaic tiles have smooth faces, their backs may differ in some respects. Some are evenly grooved, while others are finely grooved and slightly indented at the centre. Different kinds may be used together, provided they are of equal thickness.

Soak the tiles still adhering to their paper or gauze backing in hot water before removing them. Rinse the tiles once more to remove all the adhesive and spread them out on a dry towel. Sort the tiles by colour and store them in suitable containers, such as small glass jars.

Wall and floor tiles: Be on the lookout for reject tiles with attractive colours and patterns, even if they are damaged. Try to find tiles of equal thickness and free of tile cement or adhesive.

Mirrors: Suppliers of glass and mirrors usually have mirror scraps which they give away for free. These scraps are easily cut into shapes with your tile nippers, but be sure to wear gloves and goggles when performing this task. Some outlets, for example bead shops, stock mirror tiles which have already been cut into shapes suitable for mosaic.

Glass: Attractive items – such as our wine cooler – can be made from coloured glass, which is available from specialists in lead glass and suitable for outdoor use. When working with glass on glass, where both are transparent, the adhesive has to be chosen with care; we used a clear silicone adhesive. Glass lumps are also available and can be used together or combined with other mosaic tiles. You can create your own coloured glass by painting plain glass with glass paint and cutting it into pieces. Shards of glass from wine bottles can be used to great effect – as for our plant pot – but watch out for splinters and use the embedment method to cover up the sharp points.

Shells: Shells cost nothing, and collecting them is a hobby in itself. They lend themselves to beautiful projects, but bear in mind that they are too porous for grouting to be done in the normal way. It is best to embed the shells in cement or grout. The shells' cavities may be filled with Flex tile adhesive.

Porcelain shards: You can create stunning abstract items and patterns from a broken plate or two. Keep all your broken or cracked porcelain, ask your friends for theirs, and look for bargains in secondhand shops and fleamarkets. All you need are your tile nippers for cutting these items into smaller pieces. Sort the pieces by colour and keep all the smaller pieces for filling in gaps.

Found objects: Any hard objects that can be stuck down, for example beads, buttons and pebbles, may be used for mosaic.

Other requirements

Make inquiries at your nearest tile or hardware shop about the wide variety of manufacturers and brands of tiling requirements on the market. It is advisable, however, not to mix them; rather stick to one brand for the best results.

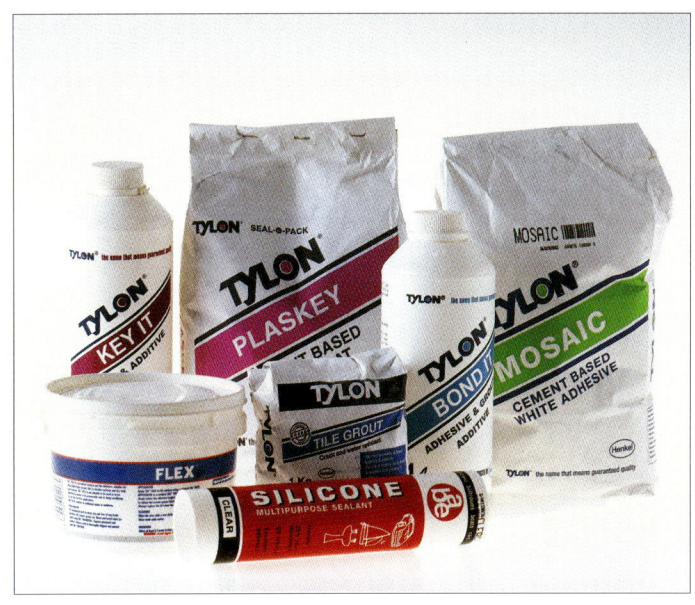

Tile adhesive: We mostly used Flex tile adhesive, which is suitable for most surfaces and for both indoor and outdoor use. This adhesive comes in small buckets, but we do not recommend working straight from the bucket as the adhesive starts to thicken very quickly. We transferred some adhesive to a small margarine tub, as well as to a squeeze bottle with a sharp spout for small spaces. Hobby shops stock such bottles, but even empty hair colourant or red plastic tomato sauce bottles work just as well.

Instant cold glue is also suitable for indoor projects, but takes longer to dry and has less gripping power. Both Flex tile adhesive and cold glue are white and become transparent when set.

Grout: This is used to fill all the blank spaces in mosaic. Grout is available in a wide range of colours, which enables you to select the one best suited to your colour scheme and design. It comes in powder form and is mixed with water or a waterproofing liquid before use. (For waterproofing an article, see p.14.) You will notice that light grey grout has been used for many projects in this book, mainly because it creates a soft effect and sets off the design beautifully. When mixing grout it is very important to follow the manufacturer's instructions closely;

the ratio is 1 part liquid to 3 parts grout. (See our step-by-step description on page 22) You can also colour grout by mixing powdered paint with the dry powder before adding the liquid. If the grout has been mixed already, watercolour in the desired shade may be added.

Bond It: This is a milky liquid which is added to grout or mosaic cement to waterproof it. Again, follow the manufacturer's instructions carefully – mix 3 parts grout with 1 part *Bond It*. Since this product is glue-based, you will have a hard time cleaning the tiles if you use too much. In that event, rub the tiles clean with a rag moistened with lacquer thinner.

Key It and *Plaskey*: These two products are brushed onto very smooth and awkward surfaces such as plastic, porcelain and metal, enabling you to apply mosaic to these surfaces. Mix them to the manufacturer's instructions, i.e. 1 part *Plaskey* to 1,5 parts *Key It*. You will notice that the mixture resembles a dark grey cement paint with a granular texture. Leave to dry for 24 hours before starting the mosaic. When in doubt about a surface, the golden rule is to consult the experts at your tile shop. If you are still unsure, use *Key It*.

Silicone adhesive: We used this mainly for sticking glass to glass, and found that squeezing out lines of adhesive onto the background surface worked much better than applying it to each individual shard or lump of glass.

Household tile cement: This is a grey powder which can be mixed with either water or a waterproofing liquid. Use 3 parts cement to 1 part water. As it is used mainly for general tiling of large surfaces such as floors and walls it comes in large packs only, although kilogram packs are available at some hardware shops. It is particularly suitable for the embedment method.

Mosaic cement base white adhesive: This product, a powder, is used mostly for mosaic in swimming pools. It is mixed with water or a waterproofing liquid (*Bond It*) and can also be used for grouting. Follow the manufacturer's instructions carefully when mixing this adhesive. Mix 2,5 parts cement powder with 1 part water or *Bond It* and allow 10 minutes for it to reach a gel-like consistency. Stir again and apply. Do not add more water. It is also suitable for the embedment method, which was used for our terracotta pot with glass shards. For hobby projects we recommend *Flex* tile adhesive.

Tools

Tile nippers: Although there are various kinds available for cutting mosaic tiles, we used curved-nose nippers for all the projects in this book. With these nippers you can nibble away small pieces, cut a tile in half or, once you have become more proficient, quarter the tile in an instant. It is important to place the tile in

the exact centre of the nippers to ensure a neat result. Less effort is needed if you grip the curved part of the handles when cutting a tile. You will find that some tiles can be cut easily and cleanly, while others splinter and fly all over the place. Do not lose heart when this happens – simply pick up all the pieces and keep them for filling the gaps around designs.

Hammer: An upholsterer's hammer, with a sharp point on one side, is required for breaking up large shards of glass or tiles. Place the materials in a strong bag to prevent the small pieces from flying all over.

Goggles: Protect your eyes against splinters, especially when cutting mirrors and glass.

Dust mask: Grouting produces very fine dust particles, making it essential to wear a mask to avoid breathing them in.

Plastic and latex gloves: Since grout and cement corrode the skin, and it is sometimes necessary to smooth the surface with your fingers, gloves are essential. Besides, dark-coloured grout will dirty your fingernails and stain your skin. Also wear gloves when working with glass.

Dough scraper: With this pliable tool you can work grout into the smallest gaps. Tile scrapers are also available at tile and hardware shops.

Sponges: Use a damp sponge for wiping off excess grout.

Graph paper: This was one of our most useful aids while writing this book. The Sariegraph paper (see "List of suppliers", p. 105) has squares measuring 1 cm x 1 cm each – more or less the size of a quarter mosaic tile. Arrange and rearrange the tiles on this paper until you are satisfied with the design.

Choosing designs

When choosing or drawing your own design, bear in mind that you will be working with a coarse medium. This means that too-fine lines or detail will be lost unless the area to be covered is very large, for example a wall. Since this book is focused on smaller projects there are a few guidelines to follow.

As fine lines tend to disappear, try shading with more than one colour instead. Make a curve or spiral by cutting one side at a slight angle to form the required shape. Leave enough room between design lines: when drawing flowers, for example, remember that the background will have to be filled in with tiles of a different colour. Always leave gaps between the tiles for grouting – this is one of the outstanding characteristics of mosaic.

There are various methods of transferring your design to the base. Trace it by means of carbon paper or make a freehand drawing; white chalk may be used for drawing on a dark background. You can also cut out the design, for instance the apple and fishes in this book, and trace the outlines of the paper template on the surface.

A photocopier makes quick work of enlarging designs.

An easy way of calculating the approximate number of tiles required is to cover the entire design with whole tiles in all the various colours. Allow 1 or 2 extra tiles to replace badly cut ones.

Crisis management

As with any other craft, occasional problems are inevitable. For example, a tile might become detached because you started grouting too soon instead of allowing 24 hours for the adhesive to set. There is always a solution to any problem, however: simply remove the offending tile, taking note of its position, and complete the grouting. Carefully scrape the grout off the spot where the missing tile has been, apply a little adhesive to a clean tile and glue it down in this space. Smooth the grout around the tile with your finger and apply some more grout here, if necessary.

Getting adhesive on the upper surface of tiles is another common problem, which is easily avoided by continually wiping off any excess with soft paper or an ear bud as you work. Adhesive that has already hardened on the tiles can be removed by rubbing the surface vigorously and hard with a rag moistened with a small amount of lacquer thinner.

If you have allowed too much grout to dry on the tiles – and it really gets very hard! – you can remove it with a new sponge scourer or, in the worst cases, with fine sandpaper. Do not make matters worse, however, by scratching the tiles or dulling their surfaces. Remember that the tiles have shallow indents and grooves which automatically fill with grout – they are supposed to look like that!

Equipping your workroom

Naturally, your very first step will be to purchase all the necessary materials and tools. It is essential to set aside a separate area for this craft, as cutting the tiles can become quite messy. Soak the tiles attached to paper sheets in hot water, then rinse once again to remove all the glue. Sort the tiles by colour and store them in small glass jars. An empty ice-cream container or shoe box in which to cut the tiles is handy to have around, as it will prevent splinters from flying all over. Stepping on a splinter hurts like blazes, and if this should happen to a member of your family you will get all the blame!

Cutting techniques

Cutting the tiles in half is the very first cutting technique you will learn. Centre the tile in the nippers and apply firm, even pressure. The tile will break in half – and sometimes even into quarters – easily. Always have a few extra tiles at hand to replace those which refuse to break the way you want them to.

To cut a triangle, place the tile in the nippers at an angle (i.e. diamond-fashion).

To cut a circle, start by nibbling away the corners. It is always better to nibble away small pieces gradually than to cut off large ones all at once; the latter method will only cause the tiles to break into the wrong shapes. Keep on nibbling away the corners in this fashion until you are satisfied with the circle you have created. This technique can be applied to both whole and quarter tiles.

To cut an eye or a leaf shape (see Garden bench, p. 100), once again turn the tile at an angle (diamond-fashion) and nibble away the top and bottom corners.

You can also use a hammer if you need uneven splinters, as for the flowers on the bread bin (p. 42).

And remember the golden rule: always nibble away small pieces at a time.

Mosaic techniques

Direct method

We mostly opted for this method, which entails sticking the tiles directly onto a base on which a design has been drawn. The size of the gaps between the tiles, which will be grouted, depends entirely on you. Once filled with grout, these gaps lend additional strength to the fixed tiles and heighten the impact of the mosaic. It is also important to realise that, no matter how hard you try to imitate something, no two mosaics could ever be identical, simply because each individual brings his or her own personal touch to the work.

To apply the adhesive you will have to find the method that works best for you. We discovered that using a squeeze bottle with a thin spout to apply the adhesive to a single tile at a time, produced the best results. This method ensures that each tile receives enough adhesive for maximum gripping power. When working with whole tiles you can use an ice-cream stick, or something similar, for applying the adhesive. And for those of us who have not been blessed with much patience, squeezing adhesive all along the design lines might be the best option.

Do not move tiles that have been stuck down already, since they will lose their gripping power and require more adhesive. Tiles which have been removed and on which the adhesive has hardened should not be reused, as they will not be flush with the surrounding tiles. Do not apply too much adhesive, otherwise the excess will be forced out to the sides of the tile, form a hard ridge and hamper any filling that has to be done around the tile.

Indirect method

This method entails drawing the design on brown or graph paper and then gluing the tiles, face down, onto the paper with a water-based adhesive such as wallpaper paste. It is particularly suitable for working on a dark background, where the design cannot be traced with the aid of carbon paper. A further advantage is that you can work indoors on large projects, such as a swimming pool or our garden bench, for days on end. Since the smooth sides of the tiles are glued onto the flat paper, mosaic done in this way tends to have a very even surface.

Spread tile cement over the entire surface to be decorated. Carefully press the paper-covered tiles onto the cement and allow to dry. Remove the paper and complete the grouting. This technique requires a fair amount of practice.

Embedment method

For this method, mosaic pieces are pressed into wet cement. Mix the tile cement to the manufacturer's instructions and spread thickly over the surface to be decorated with mosaic. Press the mosaic objects into the wet cement. Obviously, the cement eliminates the need for grouting. We used this method for the shell-decorated pot (p. 94), paving slabs with pebbles (p. 82) and terracotta pot with glass shards (p. 92).

Grouting

Pull on gloves and mix the grout to the correct consistency, carefully following the manufacturer's instructions. Grout that is too thin will sink away between the tiles and form air bubbles. Leave the mixture to thicken slightly for at least 5 minutes before applying. Mix again but do not add more water.

Spread the grout over the entire mosaic area with a dough or tile scraper, pressing down quite firmly and working in all directions to fill the gaps. Wipe off the surplus but do not try cleaning the tiles properly at this stage, since the wet grout in the gaps might be wiped away as well. Leave for a while, then wipe gently with a damp sponge. Repeat after a while until the surface is clean. Leave to dry for 24 hours, and leaving the wet grout in the sun or wind will not make it dry faster!

Polish with a clean, dry cloth. After a day or two the mosaic may be washed with hot water and soap to remove all dust particles.

Step-by-step mosaic and grouting

1. Trace the pattern freehand or by means of carbon paper. Mark the position of the design carefully with light pencil lines.

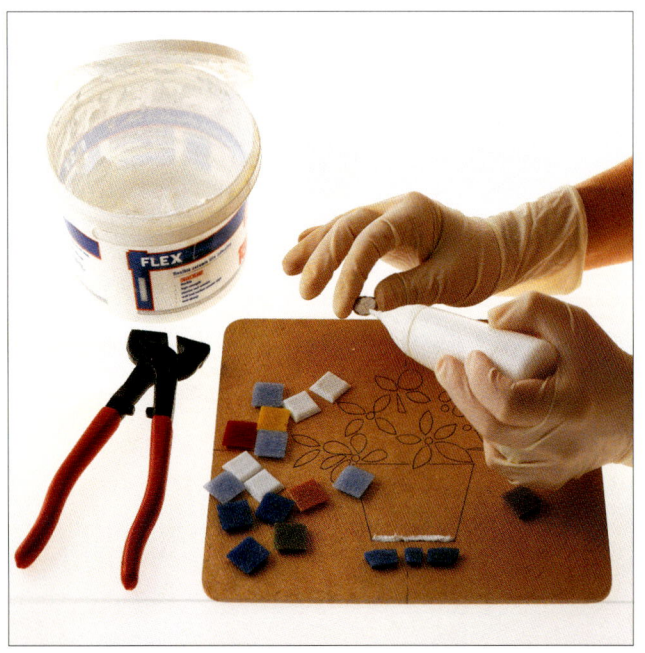

2. Cut the tiles into quarters and shapes, depending on your design. Choose the fixing method that suits you best – apply adhesive to each tile individually or use a squeeze bottle to deposit lines of adhesive on the surface. You can fill in the background in straight lines or follow the lines of the design (see Bedside cabinet, p. 72).

3. First complete the outer edge, then the traced design and, lastly, the background.

4. Leave the completed mosaic for 24 hours to allow the adhesive to dry thoroughly.

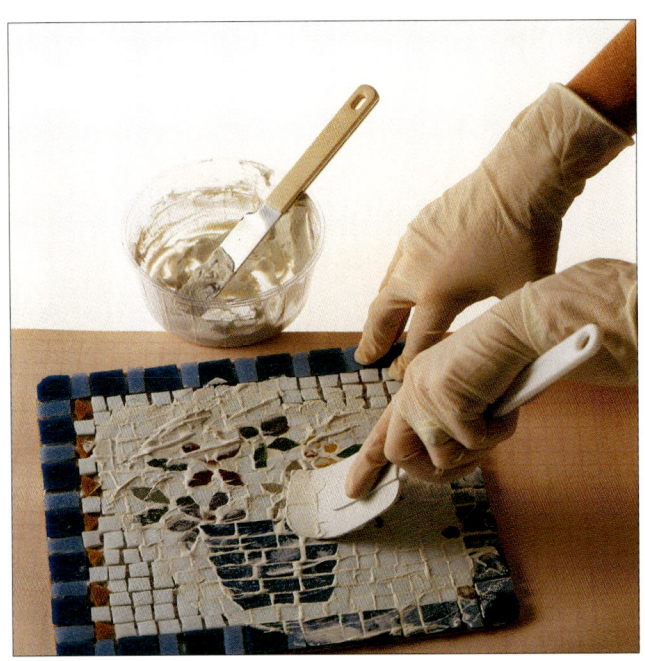

5. Mix the grout to the manufacturer's instructions, or see p. 13. Leave for at least 5–10 minutes. Apply it with a dough or tile scraper, spreading it in all directions to work it into the grooves evenly.

6. Leave for an hour or two, then wipe gently with a damp sponge. Repeat after a while until the surface is clean. Leave to dry for 24 hours.

7. Polish with a clean, dry cloth. (See also "Grouting", p. 21.)

indoor projects

box of coasters

This ridiculously easy project is ideal for beginners. Boxes of coasters such as this one are available at shops specialising in raw-wood products for hobby projects. (See "List of suppliers", p. 105.)

Requirements
box of coasters
whole mosaic tiles in different colours
Flex tile adhesive
tile nippers
grey grout
Bond It
grey paint
paintbrush

METHOD
Glue the tiles onto the lid of the box. For this project you may leave wider gaps between the tiles to avoid having to cut some of them. Next, glue tiles onto each coaster and leave to dry thoroughly.
   Mix the grout with *Bond It* to waterproof it (see p. 14) and complete the grouting (see p. 21).
   Paint the box grey and leave to dry.

checkered blackboard frame

Such a blackboard is very handy in the kitchen and an attractive addition to a nursery. This project is undoubtedly one of the easiest in the book – even a child will be able to master it. All you have to do is glue the tiles on straight; no cutting is necessary.

Requirements
1 flat wooden frame measuring 45 cm x 60 cm x 7,5 cm
116 white, 116 red and 4 black mosaic tiles
Flex tile adhesive
light grey grout

METHOD
Arrange white and red tiles alternately all along the inner edge to form an idea of how wide the gaps between the tiles should be. Using this as a guide, glue the tiles into place to complete the inner edge.

Complete the outer edge, placing white opposite white and red opposite red. Position a black tile at an angle (diamond-fashion) in each corner, ensuring that two of its corners touch the outer edge. Now complete the middle row in opposing colours (see photo). Leave to dry for 24 hours.

Mix the grout and complete the grouting (see p. 21).

two plain frames

Most hobby shops stock such plain frames. They are ideal for mosaic and enable you to practise your cutting techniques.

Requirements
2 plain raw-wood frames
white and sea-green mosaic tiles
4 glass lumps
Flex tile adhesive
tile nippers
white grout

METHOD
Square frame: Take 16 tiles and nibble off one small corner of each. Glue these tiles onto the corners of the smaller frame in such a way that the glass lumps will fit in the middle. Glue down the remaining tiles and leave the adhesive to dry. Complete the grouting (see p. 21).

Rectangular frame: Set tiles in a diamond pattern down the middle of all four sides. Cut triangles (see p. 19) to fill in the surrounding spaces. Use smaller triangles at the corners – cut them from those tiles that did not break perfectly. Leave the adhesive to dry.

Mix the grout and complete the grouting (see p. 21).

white-and-red heart

Inspired by the profusion of mosaics in our homes, one of our teenage daughters decided to make a mosaic picure of a heart for her bedroom. Cutting the tiles was plain sailing for her and she completed the project in no time at all.

Requirements
pencil and ruler
hardboard measuring 30 cm x 30 cm x 2 cm
about 70 white and 260 red mosaic tiles
Flex tile adhesive
tile nippers
white grout

METHOD
Divide the hardboard into quarters, using a pencil and ruler. Draw a heart shape in the middle of the hardboard square. Starting in the middle and using the straight pencil line as a guide, glue down the tiles for the white heart, but do not cut and glue down the tiles for the curved sides at this stage. Complete the red background, using the white tiles as a guide.

Cut white and red tiles into triangles and use to fill the gaps, completing the picture. Leave to dry for 24 hours.

Decorate all four sides with red tiles. Do this over a period of 4 days, each time placing the picture in an upright position and applying the tiles to the uppermost side. Leave to dry for 24 hours.

Mix the grout and complete the grouting (see p. 21).

plant pots

This is the perfect gift for a friend who has everything! Although the pots are small, this project is quite time-consuming. To prevent the tiles from sliding off you have to wait for the adhesive to dry before turning a pot, so work on all three pots at the same time.

Requirements
3 small terracotta pots
red, light and dark blue, yellow, green and light grey mosaic tiles
Flex tile adhesive
tile nippers
white grout
Bond It

METHOD
Lay the pots on their sides, using some kind of support to prevent them from rolling over. First complete the flowers. Cut red, blue and yellow tiles into triangles (see p. 19) for the flower petals. Cut flower centres from red and yellow tiles (they can be any shape you wish), position them in the middle and arrange the coloured triangular petals around them.

Also start gluing whole tiles (a single colour for each pot) to the rims. We chose red, blue and green edgings. Cut light grey, light blue and green tiles into smaller pieces and use them to fill in the gaps between the flowers and to cover the remaining surface. Leave the pots undisturbed for a few hours to allow the adhesive to set.

Turn the pots and repeat the process. The last tile of each of the top edgings might have to be cut smaller to make it fit into the available space. Leave to dry for 24 hours.

Mix the grout with *Bond It* (see p. 14) and complete the grouting (see p. 21).

key rack

An easy, quick and practical project. Brighten up the grey with small mirrors, placed randomly. Small mirror tiles are available, but we made our own by cutting a broken mirror into small squares.

Requirements
a small plank measuring about 14 cm x 25 cm x 2,5 cm
pencil
carbon paper
tile nippers
light and dark grey mosaic tiles
mirror fragments
Flex tile adhesive
grey grout
5 small nails
5 L-hooks

METHOD
Using a pencil and carbon paper, trace the design on p. 108 onto the plank. Cut the tiles into quarters, then cut some dark grey tiles even smaller to make the key bow. You will have to cut a few more shapes, such as small triangles (see p. 19) for shaping rounded sections. Remember to nibble away small pieces at a time when cutting a particular shape. Cut the mirror fragments into small squares, more or less the size of the mosaic tiles.

First glue down the tiles for the key design and then complete the background, placing the tiles in straight lines and inserting a small mirror here and there. Use the mirrors sparingly – the final result should not be too shiny. Place the last two rows further apart to allow for the hooks to be screwed in with ease. Leave the adhesive to dry.

Mix the grout and complete the grouting (see p. 21). While the grout is still slightly wet, tap the 5 nails gently into the wood at regular intervals to mark the positions of the L-hooks. Once the grout has dried completely, remove the nails and screw in the hooks.

dishcloth hooks

This project is done in a jiffy and makes an ideal gift.

Requirements
2 wooden rectangles, each measuring about 8 cm x 8,5 cm
white, light and dark blue, red, orange and yellow mosaic tiles
tile nippers
Flex tile adhesive
4 small nails
white grout
2 hooks

METHOD
Drill a hole at the back of each wooden rectangle so that it can be hung when completed. Mark the positions of the hook and its screws on the wood.

Cut the tiles into quarters. Complete the border with white and dark blue tiles. Cut red (or orange) flower petals and glue them down. Press yellow or black centres into place. Fill the area around the flower with light blue tiles, leaving the marked positions for the screws uncovered. Leave the adhesive to dry.

Tap the nails lightly into the wood to mark the positions of the screws. Mix the grout and complete the grouting (see p. 21). Smooth the grout around the nails with your finger. Remove the nails. Leave to dry completely before screwing down the hooks.

bread bin

The number of tiles will depend on the size of the bread bin. Only the lid is covered with tiles, otherwise the bin will become too heavy and unwieldy.

Requirements

raw-wood bread bin (see "List of suppliers", p. 105)	green and white mosaic tiles
	Flex tile adhesive
sandpaper	tile nippers
pencil and ruler	carbon paper
thin white paint	old rag
paintbrush	hammer
medium and light blue, red, yellow,	white grout

METHOD
Sand the bread bin, if necessary. Find the centre line of the lid and mark it with a light pencil line. Ensure that the bin is entirely free of dust before starting to paint. Apply two coats of paint, but leave the lid unpainted. Allow the first coat to dry thoroughly before applying the second.

Make a border of medium and light blue tiles along the edge of the lid, starting from the centre so that the cut tiles can be placed less conspicuously at the outer edge.

Enlarge the flower pattern on p. 107 to fit your bread bin, taking the border into account. Using a pencil and carbon paper, trace it onto the lid.

Place 3 red tiles on your working surface, coarse sides down, and cover them with an old rag to prevent them from flying all over the place. Tap them lightly with the hammer until they break into uneven splinters. Repeat the process with 2 yellow tiles. These tiles will form the flowers. Apply adhesive to the splinters and press them into place.

Cut 6–7 green tiles into quarters and uneven shapes and use these to make the stems and leaves. Cut some light blue tiles into quarters and use to fashion the vase. Fill the area around the design with whole white tiles. Where necessary, cut these tiles smaller for filling in and around the design.

Mix the grout and complete the grouting (see p. 21).

fridge magnets

Yet another original gift, quick to make, and a clever way of using up your splinters. Most hobby shops stock similar wooden cutouts and magnets.

Requirements
wooden shapes
tile splinters
tile nippers
Flex tile adhesive
grout
strong, round magnets

METHOD
Glue tile splinters onto the wooden shapes and leave to dry. Mix the grout and complete the grouting (see p.21). Glue magnets to the backs of the cutouts.

vases

This is a very good way of disguising cracks or chips. The vases should be glazed on the inside only. Those glazed on the outside should first be treated with *Plaskey* and *Key It* (see p. 14) before applying mosaic.

Requirements
vases of your choice
pencil
white and green (various shades) mosaic tiles
Flex tile adhesive
tile nippers
white and cream grout

METHOD

Tall, cylindrical vase: Pencil a spiral pattern from top to bottom. Draw a small leaf here and there. Quarter the tiles as neatly as possible and cut several green tiles into small leaf shapes and thin stems. Using various green shades, first complete the green stem and then the leaves. Leave to dry for 24 hours, then start gluing down the white tiles along the curve of the spiral. This project works best if the adhesive is allowed to dry in between.

Cone-shaped vase: Mark off a 5 cm border at the top (depending on the height of the vase) and one of 3 cm at the bottom. Fill in these borders with tiles in shades of green.

Mix the grout and complete the grouting (see p. 21), using white grout for the cylindrical vase and cream-coloured grout for the cone-shaped one.

fruit plate with oranges

This large, glazed plate (with a very unsightly motif) was treated with *Plaskey* and *Key It* to prepare it for mosaic. Use it as a receptacle for fruit or hang it on the wall.

Requirements

Plaskey and *Key It*	pencil
large porcelain plate	graph or brown paper
bright blue, red, orange, orange-brown, green (2 shades), white, blue and splintered black mosaic tiles	wallpaper paste
	Flex tile adhesive
	dishcloth
tile nippers	white grout

METHOD
Mix the *Plaskey* and *Key It* (see p. 14) and brush the plate with this mixture. Leave for 24 hours before starting the mosaic.

Cut all the whole tiles into quarters. Since the surface is dark the indirect method (see p. 20) is used for this project. Trace the pattern on p. 109 onto graph or brown paper.

First complete the bowl, using bright blue tiles. Use wallpaper paste to stick the tiles, grooved sides up, onto the paper. Cut the red tiles once more to make long, narrow pieces and use these to complete the scroll motif. Now make the oranges, starting with a small black piece and shading in the surrounding area with orange-brown tiles. Complete the leaves, then allow the wallpaper paste to dry completely.

Using a squeeze bottle with a thin spout, apply a drop of tile adhesive to each tile and invert the entire design onto the centre of the plate. Leave to dry, then tear off the backing paper. Cover the design with a well-moistened (not saturated) dishcloth to soak away the remaining paper. Rub the paper off gently.

Fill in the surrounding area with white tiles, following the curves of the bowl and oranges. Cut several blue tiles once more to make narrower pieces and glue them down to make the inner edging. Cover the rim of the plate with 2 rows of white tiles and finish with a final blue edging. Leave to dry completely.

Mix the grout and complete the grouting (see p. 21).

mirrored trinket box

We gave this small, battered wooden box a new lease of life by covering it with mirrors. The areas where the mirrors will go as well as the legs and wooden edge must be sanded before applying the mosaic.

Requirements
an old trinket box
Dala gold hobby paint
12 mirror tiles, each 2,5 cm square
4 pink glass lumps
mirror fragments
tile nippers
Flex tile adhesive
white grout

METHOD
Apply gold paint to the legs and bottom edge and leave to dry.

Glue a mirror tile onto each corner of the lid, followed by one placed diamond-fashion in the centre of the lid with a glass lump at each corner, and another placed diamond-fashion next to each glass lump. Fill the surrounding area with mirror fragments, positioning those with straight edges along the edge of the lid.

Glue 3 more mirror tiles to the front of the box, 1 in the centre and 2 at the sides. Fill in with cut mirror fragments, leaving room for the hasp. Also glue mirror fragments onto the remaining sides of the box. Finish with a row of mirror fragments along the bottom edge of the lid. Leave to dry for 24 hours.

Mix the grout and spread over the entire lid and all the sides, keeping the box tightly closed. Leave an edging of grout along the upper edge of the lid. Complete the grouting (see p. 21).

cake tin

Even metal can be decorated with mosaic, provided that it is treated with *Plaskey* and *Key It* first.

Requirements

Plaskey and *Key It*	1 red mirror tile
fairly small cake tin	*Flex* tile adhesive
white pencil crayon	masking tape
tile nippers	white grout
white, purple, yellow, cream and pink mosaic tiles	*Bond It*

METHOD

Mix the *Plaskey* and *Key It* (see p. 14) and apply to the cake tin and lid. Do not paint the part of the rim that will be covered by the lid. Leave for 24 hours before applying the mosaic.

Since the motif is small and has little detail it can be traced onto the lid with a white pencil crayon. Cut the white and purple tiles into quarters and the yellow ones into circles. Cut the cream tiles into the smallest possible shapes, ensuring at the same time that they can be handled comfortably and will offer a big enough surface for the adhesive to be applied. Cut the pink tiles into irregular shapes and the red mirror tile into a small circle to resemble a cherry. Fashion the cake with the purple, cream and pink tiles and position the "cherry" slightly off-centre. Glue down a few yellow circles around the edge of the lid and fill in the remaining area with white tiles arranged in circular rows.

Decorate the tin from the bottom to the top, starting with a row of yellow circles and white tiles around the bottom edge, followed by a row of purple tiles, 2 white rows and 1 purple row. Continue in this manner until you reach the part of the rim that will be covered by the lid. To keep this part free of grout, cover it with masking tape once the adhesive has dried completely.

Mix the grout with *Bond It* (see p. 14) and complete the grouting (see p. 21).

teaspoon holder

Put the teaspoons in a tin like this when serving coffee.

Requirements
Plaskey and *Key It*
clean jam tin
sandpaper
exterior varnish
tile nippers
leftover tiles
Flex tile adhesive
white grout
Bond It

METHOD
Mix the *Plaskey* and *Key It* (see p. 14) and apply to the outside of the jam tin. Sand the inside of the tin with a few quick strokes of the sandpaper. Apply 2 coats of exterior varnish to the inside to prevent rust, leaving it to dry thoroughly between coats.

Cut the tiles into quarters (we used leftover tiles) and glue them onto the tin in rows of any colour.

Mix the grout with *Bond It* (see p. 14) and complete the grouting (see p. 21).

wine cooler

This is an easy project, but requires some patience. Since the surface is rounded only a small area can be covered at a time, otherwise the glass lumps will slide off. This wine cooler can also serve as a candle holder (for tea candles).

Requirements
cylindrical glass wine cooler
Prestik
clear silicone adhesive
green and amber glass lumps
smaller, bright orange glass lumps
terracotta-coloured grout
Bond It

METHOD
Lay the cooler on its side, supporting it with two lumps of Prestik to keep it steady. Place a drop of silicone adhesive on each glass lump and work from the bottom to the top of the cooler, starting with 2 rows of green glass lumps. Make the flower row by gluing down 4 amber lumps and placing a smaller, bright orange lump in the middle. Repeat the process to complete the row, then follow with more green rows. Continue in this manner until the entire surface has been covered. Leave for 24 hours before applying the grout.

Mix the grout with *Bond It* (see p. 14) and complete the grouting (see p. 21).

jug with olives

This old, badly chipped jug was found hidden in a cupboard and transformed into a favourite vase.

Requirements
Plaskey and *Key It*
an earthenware or porcelain mug
white pencil crayon
brown, olive-green, grey and purple mosaic tiles
tile nippers
Flex tile adhesive
grey grout
Bond It

METHOD
Mix the *Plaskey* and *Key It* (see p. 14) and apply the mixture to the entire surface, except the handle. Leave to dry for 24 hours.

Using the white pencil crayon, trace the pattern on p. 108 onto the front of the jug. Draw a line 3 cm from, and parallel to, the rim of the jug.

Cut the brown tiles into long pieces for the stems and brown borderline. Cut eye shapes and slightly irregular circles for the leaves (see "Cutting techniques", p. 19) and cut the grey tiles into quarters.

First make the stem, followed by the brown borderline near the rim of the jug. Fill in the rest with grey tiles. Leave the adhesive to dry.

Mix the grout with *Bond It* (see p. 14) and complete the grouting (see p. 21).

place mat

This project will show you how to shade with small pieces of mosaic tiles. Find inspiration by studying coloured diagrams in books on cross-stitch embroidery, but bear in mind that you will use far fewer pieces than there are squares in these diagrams. You can also draw and colour in the fruit on graph paper.

Requirements
a hardboard place mat (see "List of suppliers", p. 105)
various shades of green, grey, brown, orange, yellow and red mosaic tiles
tile nippers
Flex tile adhesive
white grout
Bond It

METHOD
Draw a simple fruit (such as the apple in the photo) in the centre of the place mat as well as on paper. Using your colour drawing as a guide, start cutting small pieces in these colours and arrange and rearrange them on the paper sketch until you are satisfied with the shading.

Start by gluing down the tiles for the outlines of the apple. Complete the inner section, followed by the leaf stem and the leaf. Create a border by alternating whole green and light grey half tiles. Nibble away one corner of a green tile for each of the rounded, outer corners. Cut light and darker grey tiles into smaller pieces and fill in the area around the apple. Relieve the solid grey of the surface with small green pieces placed randomly.

Mix the grout with *Bond It* (see p. 14) and complete the grouting (see p. 21).

towel hooks with shells and frame

Requirements

- a small plank measuring 15 cm x 50 cm and about 2 cm in width
- pencil
- graph paper
- shells
- pink, white and pale yellow shards of glass
- tile nippers
- 3 hooks
- 6 screws
- matches
- ivory-coloured grout
- *Bond It*
- dough scraper
- light and dark grey and light and dark coral mosaic tiles, about 25 of each colour
- *Flex* tile adhesive

METHOD

Rack: Trace the outlines of the plank onto the graph paper, indicating the positions of the hooks. Arrange the shells in an attractive pattern on the paper. Cut the shards of glass into squares and arrange in a square pattern around the shells in the middle to serve as an accent.

Position the hooks equidistant from one another on the plank and drill holes for the screws. Screw the hooks down lightly and trace their outlines. Remove the hooks and insert a match into each screw hole.

Mix the grout with *Bond It* (see p. 14) and coat the entire front of the plank with this mixture, using a dough scraper or a large spatula to achieve an even surface. Scrape away the grout around the matches until the pencilled outlines of the hooks are visible. Screw the hooks into position.

Apply a little grout to the cavities of the shells. Working carefully and keeping your hands clean, gently press all the shells and pieces of glass into the grout according to the pattern you created on paper. Leave the plank in a horizontal position for 24 hours.

Using the Flex tile adhesive, cover the outer edge with mosaic tiles in various colours. It is best to do this over a period of 4 days, so that each side can be left to dry undisturbed. Lastly, fill the gaps between the tiles with the ivory-coloured grout (see p. 21).

Picture frame: Select mosaic and glass tiles in the same colours as the shells and cut them into smaller squares. Cover the entire front of the frame with these tiles and fill in the gaps with grout.

bathroom box

Bathrooms rarely have enough storage space, so make or buy a wooden box like this one and store all your bathtime goodies in there.

Requirements
a wooden box of your choice
white oil paint
paintbrush
pencil
bright blue, sea-green, white and light grey mosaic tiles
tile nippers
Flex tile adhesive
white grout
Bond It

METHOD
Waterproof the box by applying 2 to 3 coats of oil paint to the inside and bottom. Leave to dry.
   Draw a simple, wavelike pattern on the box. Cut the tiles into quarters. Use the bright blue and sea-green tiles for the wavelike pattern and fill in the surrounding area with white and grey tiles. Leave to dry.
   Mix the grout with *Bond It* to waterproof it (see p. 14) and complete the grouting (see p. 21).

tissue holder

It is advisable to decorate the lid only, otherwise the walls of the box will become too thick and project beyond the edge of the lid. Here we practised cutting tiles into circles, and combined various shades of blue, green, grey and purple with several glass lumps and beads.

Requirements
a ready-made wooden tissue holder
tile nippers
various blue, green, grey and purple mosaic tiles
light and dark blue glass lumps and beads
Flex tile adhesive
cement-coloured *Plascon Velvaglo*
paintbrush
light grey grout

METHOD

Cut several circles from each colour (see p. 19) and arrange them at random on the lid. The circles need not be the same size. If a too-large piece breaks off, keep it for filling in gaps between the circles. Arrange the glass lumps in between.

Now start gluing down the circles, bearing in mind that they consist mainly of the central, indented part of the tile; this means that you should apply enough adhesive to bring them level with the pieces used to fill the gaps. Squeeze a small amount of adhesive onto each bead and press into place. Leave to set for 24 hours. Meanwhile, paint the holder light grey and leave to dry.

Mix the grout and complete the grouting (see p. 21). Smooth the grout around the opening while still wet.

bathroom mirror

This mirror was made from a mirror fragment and a frame of compressed wood. The tiles, which we discovered in a storeroom, must be all of 20 years old. Adapt the colour scheme to match that of your bathroom; sheets of tiles in mixed colours are available from tile shops.

Requirements

compressed wood measuring 36 cm x 39 cm x 2 cm (you may, of course, change the measurements to suit your requirements)	brown (various shades) mosaic tiles
	mustard-yellow oblong and whole mosaic tiles
	2 small, yellow glass lumps
jigsaw	cream-coloured grout
pencil	*Bond It*
tile nippers	oil paint or varnish
green (2 shades) mosaic tiles	2 eye screws
Flex tile adhesive	

METHOD
Using the jigsaw, cut a 15 cm square opening about 10 cm from the upper edge, i.e. not in the middle of the frame. Trace the pattern on p. 111 onto the frame. Cut the tiles into quarters, then cut each quarter in half.

First complete the upper green scroll with a glass lump at its centre, then repeat the process for the bottom scroll, using quarter tiles and a second glass lump. Fashion the two leaves in shades of green and complete the border, alternating oblong and whole mosaic tiles. If oblong tiles are unavailable, use whole mosaic tiles only.

Fill in the areas around the scroll and leaf motifs with two curved rows. Continue in straight rows until the entire surface has been covered. Cover the inner edge of the mirror opening as well as the outer edge with tiles, sealing the entire frame in tiles.

Mix the grout with *Bond It* (see p. 14) and complete the grouting (see p. 21). Coat the back of the mirror with oil paint or varnish to waterproof it. Screw the eye screws into the frame before hanging the mirror.

butler's tray

This tray was decorated with quarter tiles and finished with an edging of whole tiles.

Requirements
large raw-wood tray (see "List of suppliers", p. 105)
white paint
paintbrush
pencil and ruler
carbon paper
white, light grey, green, dark green, purple and light blue mosaic tiles
1 or 2 yellow and red mosaic tiles for flower centres and accents
Flex tile adhesive
tile nippers
white grout

METHOD
Paint the rim of the tray white and leave to dry. Find and mark the centre of the tray. Trace the leaf pattern on p. 111 in the centre, using the carbon paper. Draw a teacup in each corner, leaving enough room for the edging.

First complete the edging, using light grey and green tiles. Remember always to start such a pattern in the middle and work outwards, so that cut tiles are positioned on the outer edges and therefore less visible. Cut 15 small leaves and complete the leaf design, forming the stems with half tiles cut slightly narrower. Make a frame of purple and light blue half tiles around the leaf design.

Now start on the two light blue and two purple cups. First cut a small flower from the purple tiles for each of the light blue cups. Glue a yellow centre into place for each of the flowers, then fill in the surrounding petals.

Use light grey tiles for the inside of each cup to create a contrast and add shading in the form of three to four grey tiles beneath each cup. Shape the purple cups in the same way, but decorate them with small, red leaves. Fill in the background with white tiles, cut into quarters. Leave to dry thoroughly.

Mix the grout and complete the grouting (see p. 21).

bedside cabinet

A fresh coat of paint and brightly coloured mosaic gave an old, weathered bedside cabinet a new lease of life.

Requirements
old bedside cabinet
sandpaper
white paint
paintbrush
pencil
red, orange, green (2 shades) and white mosaic tiles
Flex tile adhesive
tile nippers
wide masking tape
white grout

METHOD
Sand and paint the cabinet, except the part to be decorated with mosaic. Trace the pattern on p. 110 in the centre of the cabinet door.

Use whole tiles to make a border around the design, placing a green tile in each corner. Cut the remaining tiles into quarters and use to complete the design. Fill in the background with quarter tiles, working from the inside outwards and following the outlines of the design. Leave to dry.

Shield the mosaic with masking tape before applying the grout. Mix the grout and complete the grouting (see p. 21).

mosaic chair

If you have a broken chair in your storeroom and a dark and drab corner in your home begging to be brightened, this project could be an interesting solution. A quilting pattern inspired this design.

Requirements
compressed wood, large enough for the chair seat
pencil
graph paper
all your leftover mosaic tiles
Flex tile adhesive
tile nippers
grey grout
wood glue

METHOD
Trace the outlines of the existing chair seat onto graph paper and ask a carpenter to cut a seat to this pattern. If the seat is still in good condition, however, the mosaic can be applied to it directly. Starting in one corner, draw small curves freehand.

Cut all the tiles into quarters and sort by colour. Mix some of the colours to create a shaded area here and there.

Start applying the mosaic in one corner, keeping the shades together. Complete the design and leave to dry. Use wood glue to glue the seat onto the chair.

Mix the grout and complete the grouting (see p. 21).

outdoor projects

glass on glass

Coloured glass lends itself to the most beautiful mosaic designs. Glass scraps are available from some glass shops specialising in coloured glass. If you do not have access to such a shop, transform plain window glass with glass paints in various colours and use that instead. Glass is cut in the same way as tiles; in fact, it is much easier to cut.

Requirements
shallow glass jars (e.g. cheese spread jars)
shards of glass
clear silicone adhesive
black grout

METHOD
Clean the glass jars thoroughly. Cut the shards of glass into smaller pieces and glue them to the jars according to your own design. We applied the silicone adhesive directly to the surface of each jar because the pieces of glass were small and irregularly shaped. Leave to dry overnight.
    Mix the grout and complete the grouting (see p. 21).

black-and-white checkered plant pot

This is the perfect way to breathe new life into a plastic plant pot. Once the surface has been prepared the decorating itself will go quickly. The pot has to be hard and virtually inflexible; if the plastic is too thin the tiles will come off.

Requirements
Plaskey and *Key It*
sturdy plastic pot
black and white mosaic tiles
Flex tile adhesive
tile nippers
white grout
Bond It

METHOD
Mix the *Plaskey* and *Key It* according to the manufacturer's instructions (see p. 10 about using these products on awkward surfaces). Coat the entire pot with this mixture and leave to dry for 24 hours.

Starting with the rim of the pot, which will serve as your guide row, apply adhesive to each tile and press it down firmly. Allow a few minutes' drying time at regular intervals to prevent the tiles from sliding out of position. Since the pot narrows towards the bottom you will occasionally have to cut certain tiles. Try to cut the white tiles only, because it is much easier to nibble away small pieces from these than from the black ones, which tend to splinter or break into quarters. Make sure that you stick to the check pattern by referring to your guide row as you work. Complete the check pattern and leave to dry for 24 hours.

Mix the grout with *Bond It* to waterproof it (see p. 14) and complete the grouting (see p. 21).

paving slabs with pebbles

Nurseries sell paving slabs in a variety of shapes and sizes. We bought plain, thick, square slabs and decorated them with pebbles and small slate tiles. Flat pebbles work best. You can also cast your own cement slabs, provided they are thick enough to be stepped on.

Requirements
3 paving slabs, each measuring about 25 cm square
pebbles in various colours and shapes
12 slate tiles, each measuring 5 cm square
about 2 kg grey tile cement
Bond It
sponge

METHOD
Arrange and rearrange the pebbles and slate tiles into patterns on the slabs until you are satisfied with the design. Be sure to include pebbles in colours which will form a contrast with the grey cement. Remove the pebbles and tiles and arrange them into the same design next to the slabs.

Mix the tile cement with *Bond It* (see p. 14) and spread the mixture thickly over the top of each slab. Embed a slate tile at each corner, then press the pebbles into place, working carefully and keeping your hands clean throughout. Wipe around the outer edges with a damp sponge to smooth the cement and leave indoors to dry.

plate with porcelain shards

Two beautiful, antique plates, which had broken, were cut into into smaller pieces to create a new plate. We used an unglazed plate, but any plate that has been treated with a mixture of *Plaskey* and *Key It* is suitable. Since unglazed bisque is very brittle and breaks easily it should be fired once in a kiln to strengthen it.

Requirements
porcelain shards
1 unglazed plate
tile nippers
1 kg grey tile cement
sponge
dove-grey grout (optional)

METHOD
Cut the porcelain shards into smaller pieces with the nippers. Since porcelain is quite porous and easy to cut, you do not need a hammer to break it. Arrange the shards on the plate, placing the flat pieces on the level parts of the plate and the rounded pieces in the hollow section. Transfer the pieces in the same sequence to a clean sheet of paper next to the plate.

Mix the tile cement (see p. 14) and spread it thickly and evenly over the front of the plate. Embed the shards in the cement, starting in the centre of the plate and working outwards in circles towards the edge. Dab the cement forced out between the shards with a damp sponge to level it. Leave the plate for a while, then wipe the outer edge for a smoother, neater effect. Wipe the shards clean and leave for 24 hours for the cement to set.

If preferred, you can mix a little grey grout and spread it between the shards (see p. 21). The tile cement has a fairly coarse texture, while the grout will lend a smoother appearance more appropriate for porcelain. Polish the shards with a cloth once the grout has dried completely.

birdbath

Soft pastels, coupled with a small mirror here and there, were used to decorate this birdbath.

Requirements
cement birdbath
carbon paper and a ballpoint pen (the lead
of a pencil will break on the coarse surface)
light blue and sea-green (various shades), brown,
green (2 shades) and light grey mosaic tiles
1 red, 1 pink and 1 black mosaic tile for the eye, beak and breast
a few mirror tiles
Flex tile adhesive
tile nippers
grey grout
Bond It

METHOD

Trace the pattern on p. 109 with carbon paper. First complete the inner edge of the birdbath with whole tiles in shades of light blue and sea green. Cut brown tiles into long pieces and shape the long branch on which the bird is perched. Be sure to apply enough adhesive to these small pieces.

Shape the bird next: Cut a small triangle for the beak and a small circle for the eye and glue these pieces down first, followed by two quarter tiles for the breast. Cut a few light blue and sea-green tiles for the body and tail, shading them as well as possible. For example, use a dark sea green for the wing, a lighter shade for the head and two or three shades for the tail. Position the quarter tiles for the tail diamond-fashion. Fill the gaps with small triangles and splinters until you have achieved the desired effect.

Complete the branches and leaves. Fill in the background in circles, adding a small mirror here and there. Leave to dry for 24 hours.

Mix the grout with *Bond It* (see p. 14) and complete the grouting (see p. 21).

house number

Such a number at your front door will be a real eye-catcher. The size of the hardboard base will depend on the number; a double-digit number, for example, will require a wider base. Weatherproof it with a coat of waterproof varnish before starting on the project.

Requirements
a piece of hardboard, large enough to accommodate
your house number as well as a mosaic border
mirror fragments
blue and turquoise (various shades) mosaic tiles
tile nippers
Flex tile adhesive
black grout
Bond It

METHOD
Write your house number in the centre of the hardboard base, leaving enough room on all sides for a border consisting of two rows of tiles. Cut off small pieces of mirror and place them on the lines of the number. Cut triangular pieces for curved lines. Glue these pieces down with tile adhesive.

Make the outer border: Glue down a dark blue tile in each corner and in the middle of each side, flanked by a narrow mirror on either side. Complete the border with alternating blue and turquoise tiles. Complete the inner border with bright and light turquoise tiles.

Select a number of tiles in the lightest shades, cut them into quarters and glue these down in all the gaps in and around the number. Leave to dry for 24 hours.

Mix the grout with *Bond It* (see p. 14) and complete the grouting (see p. 21).

herb trough with crazy mosaic

An old, cracked cement trough has been made serviceable again. Combine broken wall tiles with a few tiles that you yourself painted and had fired. It is advisable to use tiles of equal thickness.

Requirements

cement trough	hammer
Plaskey and *Key It*	gloves
3 raw bisque tiles (see "List of suppliers", p. 105)	tile nippers
	about 2 kg grey tile cement
pencil	sponge
green porcelain paint and fine brush	dark grey grout
a variety of coloured wall tiles	*Bond It*
sturdy bag	

METHOD

Clean the trough thoroughly. Mix the *Plaskey* and *Key It* (see p.14). Paint the inside and outside of the trough with this mixture (paying special attention to the cracks) and leave to dry for 24 hours.

Draw a simple design on each raw tile with a pencil, then paint over the lines with porcelain paint. Have the tiles glazed and fired in a kiln.

Place the wall tiles in a bag and break them into smaller pieces with a hammer. Do not use too much force, otherwise they will break into a thousand tiny fragments. Pull on gloves and cut the pieces into usable shapes.

Mix about one-third of the tile cement (see p.14) and spread over the front of the trough. Apply a little cement to the backs of the small, painted tiles and position them in the middle of the trough's front. Fill the remaining area as well as the other three sides of the trough with tile shards. Using a damp sponge, wipe off any cement forced out between the shards. Leave to dry for 24 hours.

Mix the grout with *Bond It* (see p. 14) and complete the grouting (see p. 21). Once dry, the grout will be more or less the same colour as the cement. Wipe the upper edges carefully with a damp sponge for a neat effect.

terracotta pot with glass shards

Although decorating the pot is a fairly quick process, be sure to cut enough pieces of glass before you start. The cement dries quite quickly, and once you have started there can be no interruptions. The embedment method (see p. 21) is the easiest way of sticking glass shards to an object.

Requirements

terracotta plant pot	tile nippers
blue and several green wine bottles as well as glass fragments	masking tape
	mosaic cement base white adhesive
	dough scraper
sturdy bag	sponge
gloves	

METHOD

Place one bottle at a time in the bag and break with the hammer. Pull on gloves and spread out the pieces in a large, shallow carton. Pick out pieces that broke cleanly. Nibble away sharp points and cut big pieces smaller until you have more than enough. Pieces that are too rounded, for example the neck sections of the bottles, are not suitable because the pot is much less rounded.

If you wish to retain the terracotta rim, cover it with masking tape. Mix the cement to the manufacturer's instructions (see p.14) and leave for 5–10 minutes until it reaches a gel-like consistency. Do not add more water, and stir once again.

Invert the pot. Using a dough scraper and working from top to bottom, apply a strip of cement thickly and evenly. Embed the glass shards as deeply as possible. Flatten and smooth the cement that is forced out between the shards with a damp sponge before starting on the next row of shards. Continue on both sides of this row to avoid ending up at the first strip you applied, which might be partially set by that time. Leave the pot for 10 minutes, then smooth and neaten the cement around the bottom with a sponge. Also dab any uneven areas between the shards with the sponge.

Carefully turn the pot right side up and remove the masking tape. Wipe the rim to achieve a neat effect. Invert the pot once again onto clean paper and press down firmly any shards that may have become detached at the bottom. Wipe the glass shards clean carefully. Leave the pot upside down for 24 hours to allow the cement to set.

shell-decorated pot

Shells in various colours look stunning set in grey cement. Surfaces decorated in this way are never grouted, however, because the grout will stain the porous shells. The embedment method used here requires no grouting – the grey cement serves a dual purpose in this case. Make sure that you have enough shells before tackling the project.

Requirements
an old plant pot
Plaskey and *Key It*
about 3 kg grey tile cement
a variety of shells
dough scraper
sponge

METHOD
Wash and dry the pot thoroughly. Mix the *Plaskey* and *Key It* (see p. 14) and paint the entire pot, including the inside of the rim, with this mixture. Leave to dry for 24 hours.

Meanwhile, mix a little grey cement and fill all the shells' cavities. Mix a fairly large quantity of cement (see p.14) in a clean ice-cream container. Invert the pot and, using a dough scraper, spread the cement over its widest part.

Apply a small amount of cement to the shells once again, because the cement in the filled cavities usually subsides as it dries. First press the largest shells into place to form a row around the pot. Repeat the process, working alternately upwards and downwards from this first row. Smooth the cement between the shells frequently by dabbing it with a damp sponge, taking care not to dirty the shells. Dried cement is impossible to remove, so wipe the shells clean as you work.

Leave for 10 minutes, then smooth the cement around the bottom. Leave the pot upside down for 24 hours to allow the cement to set. Do not turn it over in this time, as this might cause some of the bottom shells to loosen.

Turn the pot right side up and repeat the rows of shells on the inner rim.

sconce

Requirements

a 2 cm thick plank (see the sketch on p.108)	32 red beads
an 8 cm square piece of wood (this is the platform on which the candle will rest)	3 glass lumps
	dark blue and light and dark green mosaic tiles
nail	smaller mirror fragments
cold glue	*Flex* tile adhesive
4 mirror tiles, each 2,5 cm square	tile nippers
8 red mirror tiles, each 2 cm square (Bead Merchants of Africa)	dark grey grout

METHOD

Drill two holes in the back of the plank, each 8 cm from a side and 18 cm from the bottom edge. Drive a nail through the centre of the platform to hold the candle. Place one side of the platform – with the point of the nail facing up – over the two holes and glue it to the plank with cold glue. Secure it properly with two screws inserted through the holes from the back.

Draw a vertical line down the centre of the large plank and divide it into equal sections by drawing horizontal lines. Use these lines as a guide to glue down the mirror tiles diamond-fashion, spacing them evenly as shown in the photo. Stick a bead to each corner of the red mirror tiles, and glue down two glass lumps between the three top mirror tiles and one below the bottom mirror tile.

Make an edging with dark blue tiles, positioning them diamond-fashion and ensuring that their points do not touch; the gaps in between are needed for grouting. Note that the blue tiles at the top, except the uppermost one, are not placed diamond-fashion. Fill the gaps between these tiles with narrow, oblong mirrors and the triangular gaps with triangular mirrors.

Fill the remaining surface with green tiles, alternating the shades. Use whole tiles as far as possible, cutting them only when necessary. Leave to dry for 24 hours.

Decorate the outer edges of both the platform and the backboard with whole green and blue half tiles. It is advisable to complete the backboard's edge over a period of a few days so that each side can be left to dry undisturbed. Glue a few green shards onto the top of the platform.

Mix the grout and complete the grouting (see p. 21).

poolside table
Design adapted from the Dutch magazine, *Libelle*

On discovering this old, Portuguese mosaic fish design we simply had to use it. The project requires a fair amount of skill and patience.

Requirements

a 55 cm square table	of another blue
sandpaper	(buy more than enough of each
white enamel paint	colour)
paintbrush	tile nippers
pencil	3 glass lumps
carbon paper	Flex tile adhesive
mosaic tiles: white, dark and light	white grout
blue as well as 4 shades	*Bond It*

METHOD

Sand the table, then paint the sides and legs with white enamel paint. Use a photocopier to enlarge the pattern on p. 112 to fit the table top. Trace it onto the table using carbon paper, or cut out the fishes, place them on the table and trace their outlines. Draw the other lines and the eyes freehand.

Start with the outlines of the fishes: Cut long, narrow pieces from dark blue tiles and glue them down along these lines as well as the interior line of each tail. Cut some of these long pieces at an angle and use them for the fishes' mouths and the ends of their tails. Glue a glass lump onto each eye. Cut triangles from white, turquoise and light blue tiles and glue them down around the eyes, using only one colour for each eye. Cut dark blue tiles in half and glue them down along the centre line of each fish. For the remaining parts of the fishes all the tiles are cut more or less into quarters. Create a broad band of white below each centre line and a medium blue one above it. Fill in the remainder with lighter shades of blue.

Now decorate the edge of the table with alternating white and dark blue tiles, using half tiles in the same colours for the rounded part of the edge. Fill in the rest of the background with as many light blue whole tiles as possible, placing them randomly and inserting a medium blue tile here and there to provide interest. Fill the gaps with light blue tile pieces. Leave to dry for 24 hours.

Mix the grout with *Bond It* (see p. 14) and complete the grouting (see p. 21).

garden bench

In a garden not blessed with many flowers, this bench will provide a splash of colour. Choose colours that occur in nature to create a soft, soothing effect. This is an advanced project. Although we used the direct method because the weather was good, this project is perfect for the indirect method, as the bench is too heavy to be moved around.

Requirements

- a cement garden bench
- at least 2 sheets each of light and dark grey, 1 sheet of soft grey-green, bright green (2 shades), purple, light and dull pink, dull and bright orange, dull and bright yellow and red mosaic tiles
- *Flex* tile adhesive
- tile nippers
- masking tape
- light grey grout
- *Bond It*

METHOD

Alternate the light and dark grey tiles throughout. Around the outer edge, glue down three grey tiles, a grey-green and half a bright green tile for the leaf stem, repeating this sequence until the edging is complete. For the second row, cut two green leaves for each stem and glue them down with their points touching the stem. Set grey tiles between the leaves, but keep the filling-in work for later. Complete the edging with a third row of grey tiles above the leaves, including a grey-green tile directly above each leaf.

Decorate the rest of the bench with light and dark grey tiles, placing them diamond-fashion and alternating the colours. Complete a diamond-patterned inner edging with alternating light grey and grey-green tiles.

Make the flowers by cutting petals (as for the green leaves) from various colours, but reserving the bright orange and red for small, round flower centres. Distribute the flowers over the inner area and glue them down. Fill the gaps in between with as many light and dark grey whole tiles as possible, and all the blank spaces with smaller pieces. Fill the tiny gaps between the flower petals with grout only.

Protect the cement outer edge with wide masking tape. Mix the grout with *Bond It* (see p. 14) and complete the grouting (see p. 21).

round table

Mosaic provides a very durable surface and is perfect for a table top, provided that the tiles are all of equal thickness. The geometric pattern enabled us to use a large number of whole tiles, and only a few triangles had to be cut. Planning the design required a great deal of deliberation and preparation, however, which places this project in the advanced category.

Requirements

a round table	water-based adhesive
coarse sandpaper	Flex tile adhesive
varnish	tile nippers
graph paper	grout
mosaic tiles to suit your design and choice of colours	Bond It

METHOD

Sand the table top with coarse sandpaper to give the tiles gripping power. Also sand the sides and legs of the table. Join sheets of graph paper together to cover the entire table top, then cut out a circle to the exact size of the table top. Fold this circle into quarters.

Start planning your design by arranging tiles on one quarter of the paper until you are satisfied with the pattern. We made a square in the centre and surrounded it with circular panels. The tiles in some panels, as well as those around the outer edge, were placed at an angle. Leave a gap for the grout between the tiles that are placed at an angle, i.e. the points of the tiles should not touch. Using water-based adhesive, paste your tiles onto the quarter section of graph paper and refer to them as you work. Count the number of tiles required for each colour and write it down. Allow for quite a few extra tiles, especially in the colours that need to be cut. Buy all the tiles at once to ensure that they come from the same dye lots.

Mark the centre of the table top and draw lines dividing it into quarters. Measuring from the edge, draw circles for the various panels. Start gluing down the tiles from the centre, using the lines you drew as a guide. Lastly, cover the outer edge with tiles; as our table top was about 2 cm thick the edge could accommodate whole tiles. Leave to dry for 24 hours.

Mix the grout with *Bond It* (see p. 14) and complete the grouting (see p. 21).

list of suppliers

Most tile shops stock mosaic tiles, adhesives, equipment and requirements, as do your local hobby and hardware shops; these products are freely available. We used the following suppliers for the projects in this book.

MALLS TILES
Suppliers of tiles and mosaic tiles, requirements and tools.
Address: 51 Paardeneiland Road, Paardeneiland, tel. (021) 510 5500, and 3-9 Garth Road, Mayville, Durban, tel. (031) 207 6451

LOVRIC TILES
Suppliers of mosaic tiles in small quantities and on sheets.
Address: 79 7th Avenue, Maitland, tel. (021) 593 8570

PUDLO AND CASH TILES
Suppliers of mosaic tiles and materials.
Address: 288 Voortrekker Road, Maitland, tel. (021) 511 0058 and (021) 511 0108

BEAD MERCHANTS OF AFRICA
Suppliers of mirror tiles, glass lumps and beads.
Address: 223 Loop Street, Cape Town, tel. (021) 423 4687

THE HEARTH AND HOME SHOP
Suppliers of compressed wood products.
Address: Unit E7, Access Park, Kenilworth, tel. (021) 683 1149, and Honeydew Centre No. 52, Blueberry Road, Honeydew, tel. (011) 795 4015

GLASS ROOTS
Suppliers of coloured glass and specialists in lead glass.
Address: 226 Long Street, Cape Town, tel. (021) 423 0552

DALA (KV ART)
Suppliers of hobby paints and related products, available from hobby and art shops countrywide. Tel. (021) 557 8003

POT ELIZABETH
Suppliers of bisque and porcelain painting requirements.
Address: 16B Kloof Street, Cape Town, tel. (021) 424 5401

SARIE PATTERN SERVICE
Suppliers of graph paper.
Address: P.O. Box 1802, Cape Town, tel. (021) 406 2260

SUE PEDDLE CRAFT ROUTES
Suppliers of mosaic requirements.
Address: Shop U32, Kolonnade Centre, Zambezi Road, Montana, tel. (012) 528 4811 and Jakaranda Centre, tel. (012) 331 5244

DISH
Suppliers of mosaic requirements.
Address: 38 6th Street, Parkhurst, tel. (011) 447 1071

JIMNETTES
Suppliers of mosaic requirements.
Address: Shop 42, Lynnridge Mall, Lynnwood Road, Lynnwood Ridge, Pretoria, tel. (012) 361 4469

basic designs

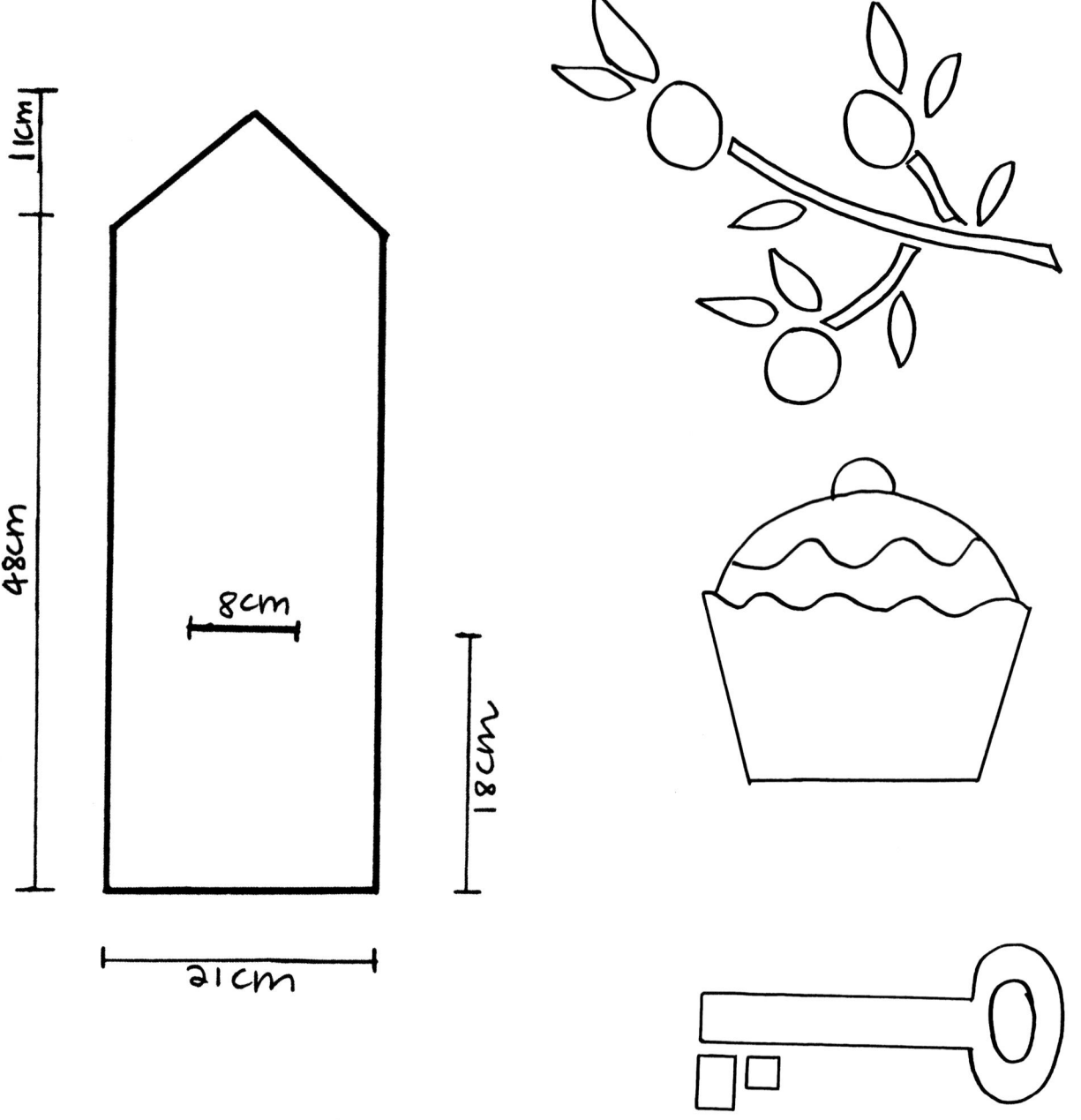

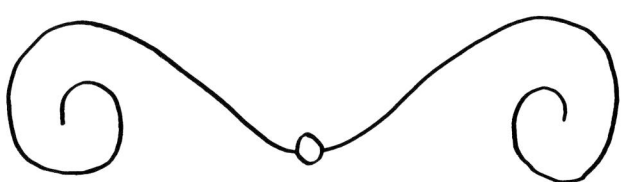
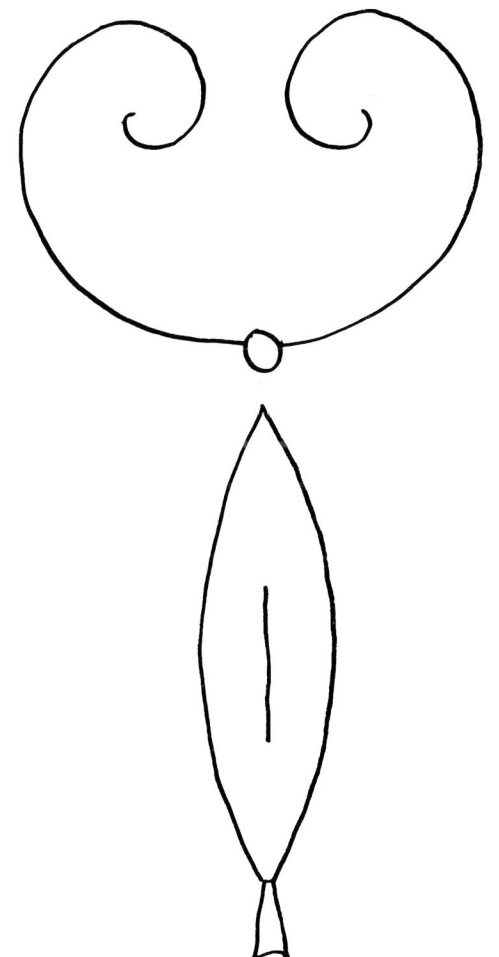